for Judy and Michael,
both of whom have always had my back

Contents

The Best of a Bad Year 13
Chevrolet Tango 14
Saved 15
La Vida Loca 16
Jimmy Olsen 17
Incredible Journey 18
Ephemera 19
Wildflowers 20
All the Time in the World 21
To Loss 22
What the Chaplain Saw 23
Namesake: An Elegy 24
Catch 25
The Bird Watcher: An Elegy 26
Livelihoods 27
The Regular 28
To Goya 29

My Presidents	30
Anecdotes	31
Nobody's	32
The End of the World Cookbook	33
Repair	36
Kairos	37
Seventieth Anniversary of the Revolution Street	38
The Widower's Daughter	39
Mixed Martial Arts	40
The Event	41
The Potato Eaterss	42
The Weekend Muses	43
A Small Thing	44
How to Become a Clown	45
Heart Like a Dog	46
Jesus H. Christ	48
Scow	49
Letting Go	50
The Unnumbered Anniversaries	51
The Correct Use of Each Other	52
Dishes	54
Drone	55
The Lost Head of the Android Philip K. Dick	56
Junkers	57
Accidents of Time and Space	58
Poem	59
The In-Joke	60
Love Poem	61
No Matter What	62
Junk	63
Cailloux	64

Signals	65
Make Like Shakespeare	67
Gnomic	68
Sixty Pieces of Word	69
More about Me	70
Note to an Old Friend	71
God on the Roof	72
Or Not	73
At a Certain Age	74
What I've Learned Living on Other Planets	75
Heron	77
Notes	79
Acknowledgments	81
About the Author	85
Title Index	87
First Line Index	91

I had a funny feeling as I saw the house disappear, as though I had written a poem and it was very good and I had lost it and would never remember it again.
—Raymond Chandler

The Unnumbered Anniversaries

Kurt Olsson

Fernwood
PRESS

The Unnumbered Anniversaries

©2025 by Kurt Olsson

Fernwood Press
Newberg, Oregon
www.fernwoodpress.com

All rights reserved. No part may be reproduced
for any commercial purpose by any method without
permission in writing from the copyright holder.

Printed in the United States of America

Page design: Mareesa Fawver Moss
Cover design: Eric Muhr
Cover art: Ajeet Mestry on Unsplash

ISBN 978-1-59498-171-5

Kurt Olsson reminds us that nostalgia is not to be trusted and that days can be measured by "after I shoved a bean up my nose / but before I gave in and walked out on my life." And yet *The Unnumbered Anniversaries* is full of small, sweet pleasures, as long as you can take comfort in the absurd, the temporary, and the grace of Willie Mays making a world-saving catch. As this collection proceeds, its expanse gets ever wilder—as if the opening poem, "The Best of a Bad Year," has set off a Rube Goldberg-ian sequence of widening chaos—and Olsson awes us with his sprightly intellect, unexpected imagery, and impeccable phrasing. Is it a big toe or a bottlenose dolphin? Yes.

—SANDRA BEASLEY
author of *Made to Explode*

Mostly brief but always poignant and well-crafted, Kurt Olsson's "many small songs to loss" in this new collection are meditations on the emotional equivalent of phantom limb syndrome. Even after a relationship has ended, Olsson reminds us, the memory and the pain remain. The catalog of experiences recounted here reads like a litany of failings: bad marriages, several jobs, and "a Wall Street deal gone bust" among them. And the ghosts materialize in varied guises, including "the dented wreck / I'd gotten / in the settlement," "a three-legged dog" in lieu of children from "a second marriage worse than the first," and "old scars / now invisible." On balance, though, the poems here are not merely confessional or mournful. For Olsson, the myriad experiences of loss add up "to a life I look back on now and wonder." The wonder lies, perhaps, in how he—or any of us—manages to survive it all but assuredly also in how we find redemption in making "what's old new again."

—MICHAEL BLANCHARD
editor of *SLANT: A Journal of Contemporary Poetry*
and author of *The Pearl Diver's Daughter & Other Poems*

In his poem "What I've Learned Living on Other Planets," Kurt Olsson writes, "Never travel with anyone who says, 'Wake me when we get there.'" Of course, such a non-companion would miss the journey, something Olsson with his imaginative wanderings, unexpected byways, and keen observations will not allow us to do. These poems, like a new landscape, challenge the way we see, often finding mystery or honor in the mundane: dishes in a tub of water become thrashing fish, the tires blown off junkers fume "like the blowsy heads of dandelions," and we are reminded of an era when bottle caps, soda cans, and pant cuffs served as ashtrays. Olsson brings us as close to the regular at the bar who "never eats anything, not even the popcorn" as he does to the carpenter who, simply trying to make a living, crafts Christ's cross or to the Russian who, once forced to burn books simply to keep from freezing, buries his nose in one he cannot read just to breathe it in. We are humbled in our understanding of how easily we could be any of them. *The Unnumbered Anniversaries* will make you laugh one moment, mesmerize you the next, and then shatter you with its forthright yet understated and empathic renderings of experiences that devastate. Still, around most every corner, we sense the poet's mission "to say what cannot but is, / and not what can be but isn't."

—Brenda Cárdenas
author of *Trace*

The Best of a Bad Year

Snowed only once
a lot
too much
to shovel out to where
I kept the kids' toboggan so I went
down to the basement
and found a moving
box big enough
and threw it in the trunk of the dented wreck
I'd gotten
in the settlement and once
the plow made it to my street I drove
to the park where kids not mine
chase balls in summer
and the three of us crunched up
to the top of a hill
the hardpack slick now
so bright it hurt and the girls
took turns in the box
they did that
until it fell apart and then
I drove them back to their mother's
I have the pictures somewhere.

Chevrolet Tango

Remember when men smoked pipes
toting around tiny tools to finesse the dottle
and the hollow *chock, chock* of meerschaum against glass,

and ashtrays the color of bourbon
one could stack as high as a basketball rim, and how
anything handy could be an ashtray—bottle top, soda can,
   pant cuff—

and lighters, monogrammed, glinting
in your hand like fool's gold, and Diamond matches
and using your thumbnail to flick a light for a friend's and only
   then your cigarette,

and don't forget mini-skirts, heat lightning slither of nylon
and strutting like cowboys, tight jeans and tighter pockets
when pockets did work, hands submerged, thumbs and all,
   like Dylan's on the cover of *Freewheelin'*,

and Colt 45 sunrises, chicken-fried steak, highways cut clean
through cornflowers, and flooding the engine to catch up
to the curve of a forearm, posed from a car window, black satin
   polish flicking ash Nile queen style.

Remember all the mistakes you wanted to make.

Saved

A warm spring evening, after the grill closes,
two guys stroll in and tell the owner
their car's broke down on the way to Topeka,
the weather's fierce, there's a tornado watch.

They ask if they can sit for a spell, dry
their unlucky bones. When that night's act
ends its set to light applause, the pair stand
and swing into the spot, easy, nonchalant, as if

one of them wasn't Black, this wasn't Iowa,
wasn't the twenty-first century. (Is that a barstool
toppling over?) Then they launch into an R&B
chestnut, softly at first, as if crouching down

to gentle a car-thrown fawn, the white guy
handling bass while the other shuts his eyes
and lets the notes unspool overhead—higher,
higher, like a fantastic, untethered bird of prey—

and everyone sets his or her blind hands down
and we all forget how to breathe for a while.

La Vida Loca

Everyone in the room, even the cats, everyone in the house,
on the street, in the neighborhood, even in the sky, all asleep.

How wonderful to wake and take a long, deep breath
and fall back to sleep to this thought. And maybe, as you try

to doze off, take it a step further: there's a tiny principality
someplace, tucked behind a mountain pass perhaps, where

citizens sleep a sleep charmed and the dreams they dream
are like booths at a country fair and one can amble about

and touch and taste the wares—fresh-baked rhubarb pie,
apples still stamped by hoarfrost, a wedge of cheddar lovingly

carved in the shape of a fire truck, booties crocheted for
those with the wit to wait until after tea to be born.

Jimmy Olsen

Why perhaps as mundane as the shared last name—
life no doubt different if born Ivanoff or Carlson.

But I'm not alone: there's an army of Jimmies
(and Janies) out there just like me.

Always the ones in pratfall, needing rescue, never
the names in all caps gracing the cover.

Sidekick, pal, wingman. The wannabe who loses himself
in a cave, gets stung by a radioactive bedbug.

The BFF with the faulty camera used as bait
to ambush the dim but dashing hero. Object, not subject.

Superpower, if any, magnified neediness, garnished
with a soupçon of envy. But given the choice,

be honest, would we Jimmies have it any other way?
Like the child at a wedding banquet

tossed in the air higher and higher by a tipsy uncle,
the thrill of being caught, the thrill of not.

Incredible Journey

I hated that dog the week it followed me
too damned to sniff out and track its legal owner.

No dog I'd ever want: paint can with paws,
toilet-brush tail widowed between its legs.

I didn't set out a water bowl or secretly scrape
leavings from my plate. I hissed and stamped—

no matter, my shadow, to school and back,
to friends', along the interstate where some

putz sideswiped it, never stopped. Up it flew
before me, executing a loop-de-loop, as if

without our knowing, fate meant it for a circus act.
What in hell did I do to earn such a death?

No last whimper, no brave pleading look, just
bared teeth, bright red splashing from its snout.

Ephemera

There was a time after I shoved a bean up my nose
but before I gave in and walked out on my life
I used to rank superheroes one to twenty-five
like the newspapers do with football teams
at number two Daredevil Black Panther eight
Batman number whatever you get the idea
I two-fingered the list on peach-colored paper my dad
brought from work why peach I don't know
on a battleship of an Olympia I did this Mondays
Hulk tumbling to twenty-three Power Girl leaping
nine spots for no reason it wasn't like they scrimmaged
one another on Saturdays like football teams do it
was just the way I guess I felt that week nonstop
color commentary brain buzz reality dictating
change it couldn't stay Spider-Man numero uno
always how long I did this who knows not so long
I hope though I wouldn't mind finding one of those lists
in an old box or tucked like a faded Polaroid nude
in the pages of a book no one's opened in forever.

Wildflowers

The first writing class told us not
what we should but what we shouldn't,
at least not until we outlived our excesses.
What was proscribed: dreams, grandparents,
ideas, our first beer, pets dead or otherwise.
In other words, most of what most of us knew well
and well enough to love. Leaving us
to apprentice on other stuff—the sky at night,
the smaller losses, the backwoods where grow
the many wildflowers of North America
whose names, to this day, I still don't know.

All the Time in the World

Though born with the fear of falling,
we humans must be taught patience.
This is why God invented fly-fishing
and macramé. When she babysat us,
she worked a pattern of Neil Armstrong
planting Old Glory on the Moon.
Neither my sister nor I ever planted
anything anywhere. Why if you use
a mallet to tenderize meat did we smack
two-by-fours to make our hands tough?
Mowing grass is pointless yet requires
patience, too. You wait for it and hope
for rain but not too much and then
up and down down and up you go
over the same sorry slab of ground.
John Cage said prehistoric people,
when they were afraid of something,
drew pictures to get over the fear.
During a Little League game, somebody's
brother raced to third base, got hit by lightning,
died. Only while you're a child
do you look up and try to count the stars.

To Loss

A young man, little more than a boy, sobs in back
of the room where tonight's poet reads
Edna St. Vincent Millay, a writer, he scolds, too much
neglected today. I've read a lot of poetry, even a little
Millay, but never been moved to tears by it,
least of all in public, at a reading, so I find myself
paying less heed to the poem than to the boy,
trying to guess what must be galling him so. What is it,
I missed, that's missing, what small part is missing
in me? I'm not alone in these thoughts, I think,
nor the only one who yearns to be transported
to a nook in a coffee shop or home in front of the TV,
anywhere but here, now. Who saves us:
a formalist in back who whispers in pure spondees,
"Shut the / fuck up."
                              Doesn't do the whole trick—
the young man's sobs dim only a bit, but it does serve
to pivot the rest of us back to the poet at the front
of the room who puts down his Millay, ready to begin
the first of his own many small songs to loss.

What the Chaplain Saw

In memory of K.A.O., 1913-1996

What he saw he never saw
and never told us.

The nakedness laid out in the ditch
not nakedness.

The darkness in every gaping mouth
not darkness.

He came back and never came back.

What he prayed to
no longer what he prayed to.

The photos he never took:
how could he save what never was?

No verb can undo nothingness.

Namesake: An Elegy

He was a punter, not the British kind, though he'd have liked that,
given his thing for all things English. He spent semesters there,
trying to outgrow his love, his first, for Chaucer. He taught me how
to hold the ball at an angle, nose down and away from one's kicking leg.
It worked, kind of, even if I punted with my left, the wrong foot.
He didn't just punt, he ran them back, too. Holds his alma mater's record
for longest runback of all time. 9/26/59. Against Lakeland.
Every few years, at moments, when I'm on standby or thinking back,
I look it up and make sure. After he had his kids, it wasn't the same,
even if they were girls. They had his hair, ginger, his faraway eyes.
My folks say I wasn't named after him, they just liked the name.
Later, he never stopped eating the wrong stuff or took good care. Suffered
the heart attack killed him during his doctor-mandated morning walk.
He ran one hundred yards that day, and no one touched him.

Catch

Without knowing you practice beauty.
The behind the back. Hard juke and feint ankle-
rolling your shadow. The sweet level swing
of hickory winched deep inside the bone.
You practice beauty with what's at hand.
Wiffleballs, friction tape, Nerf footballs,
wadded socks, Frisbees and apple cores,
spittle-slick tennis balls, homework papers
peppered red with demerits, wingnuts.
Out back, practicing the over the shoulder,
you are immortal, Willie Mays sprinting into
and through the ever after, making the catch
that saves the world, then more amazing,
plucking wonder from your glove and whipping it
home with everything you've got, like he did,
ball cap blown from your skull, your living
body splayed then spliced, like his, by joy.

The Bird Watcher: An Elegy

She loved birds, their secret logic. She went for long walks
alone, along dusty fire roads, binoculars double-strapped
about her neck. She liked believing in what might be.

After dinner, she'd sweep us all out the kitchen with her skirts
and she'd do the dishes. It wasn't a chore for her,
the silence. She had these washed-out blue eyes, like pebbles

in a streambed after a sun-shower. Sometimes
she let me go with her. Didn't talk much. Put a finger
to her lips, point up, correct more often than not.

Summers, every day, after the breakfast dishes, she rowed me
one side of the lake down the other. They're there,
she promised, but I never caught much beyond a meager bluegill.

Story goes, before my time, she posed against the doorframe
to their bedroom, in fishnets, a fedora cocked over an eye
à la Garbo, a stogie in her mouth. God, she knew how to laugh.

Livelihoods

Some carry a piece of the cross with them,
the true cross, the cross he died on, the cross
a man fashioned, the cross measured and sawed,
chiseled and fitted, the man understanding
the provenance of wood, how to work it,
what a span of wood can and cannot bear,
picturing what he was making but not
for whom, just as another might not know
for whom a hammer or lamb's shank was intended.
A man who viewed his making as a way
to earn a livelihood, the means for keeping alive,
of putting food on the table. If shavings fell
from his brow, if he pulled a splinter from a callused
thumb and it bled a little, the sawdust and blood
mixing with what was on his plate didn't alter
the taste of what he ate. Didn't make him think
of what he had or had not done that day.

The Regular

He's Bill, that's all.
No one's sweet Will.
Certainly not Billy.

If anyone calls him William,
his mother or his accountant,
if he has either. He drinks

whatever's on tap,
nothing else. Never eats anything,
not even the popcorn

and it's free. If he talks,
he smiles, embarrassed
or a mite proud he's got

an angle his own to share.
When he gives up
his barstool at last call, he stands

stock-still a few seconds,
maybe more. Shuts both eyes,
as if he needs the world

to settle inside him
or must count to make sure
his four limbs are his

and still with him. Then
he steps out into the same night
that waits for us all.

To Goya

If art is the two sons of the famous lithographer
who stole one of their father's Disasters of War prints and
 found a buyer in Dubuque, Iowa,
while he was away on holiday, whose first names were
 Leonardo
and, no shit, Michelangelo (before the mutant turtles of the
 same names),
one of whom, the fatter, hid behind the green shades of
 prescription glasses,
while the other theatrically goosed his French-accessory
 girlfriend,
who walked with their guts puffed out like butchers proud of
 the smears on their aprons,
who asked for toothpicks after dinner, as if they couldn't just
 suck their yellow teeth to unwedge
the pasta we sloshed on their plates and sold, all you can eat,
who sat for hours nursing 40 cent, bottomless cups of coffee
 and laughing,
Leonardo and Michelangelo, with their factory fresh Audis
 and reputed huge cocks—
if art is this
little wonder I'm still pissed many years later
I never tossed the dregs of their coffee back in their smiling
 faces,
never shadowed them out to the parking lot to plop, dime by
 dime, their lousy tips
onto the hand-made and brilliantly buffed Italian loafers your
 genius afforded them.

My Presidents

John F. Kennedy left me parched and sweat-soaked
on the tarmac somewhere on the Central Asia steppe,
conjugating the verb "to want." LBJ taught me how
to never give up giving up. Richard M. Nixon welshed
on refereeing the seventh-grade fistfight between me
and Tony O'Hare. Gerald R. Ford made me skip sleep
for Chevy Chase and *Saturday Night Live*. Jimmy Carter
paid for his mom not allotting him an initial he liked.
I voted John Anderson, not Ronald Reagan. Carter,
not Ronald Reagan. Mondale, not—you get my drift.
George H. W. Bush didn't do a lot I want to remember.
Bill Clinton sent me a letter impersonating Bill Clinton
thanking me for my service. George W. Bush claimed
it was over before it was over. Barack Obama paid
for my daughter's year of hospital. Donald Trump
explains my left-handedness and unease with metaverses.
Joe Biden I can't in my heart blame for much except
being the last one standing without a stool to sit on.

June 2022

Anecdotes

The first year, students would come up to me
between class while we all stood outside

the little kindergarten that had been converted
into the English faculty in the hinterlands

of the former Soviet Union and say, *Mr. Olsson,
tell us please an anecdote.* Life until then

hadn't lent itself to Chekhov, let alone Turgenev
or Tolstoy, but I'd lived a slew of anecdotes.

The students would lean in close and laugh
at the end, glancing at one another, one maybe

balling his hand in a fist and clipping a neighbor
on the shoulder, before they would thank me

and shuffle back through unlit halls painted
with ducks and dancing bears to their next class.

My second and final year, after living some more,
I came to understand when they said anecdote

they'd been taught the word meant joke,
and when asked I shook my head and told them

sorry, I didn't know any anecdotes anymore.
I always had a poor memory for such things.

Nobody's

I didn't know shit. I knew
I didn't know shit. Sad thing
I didn't care I didn't know shit.

They sent me places. Sometimes
I'd leave the hotel and walk.
Didn't know where—just walk.

I liked being in places where
I didn't know the lingo, where
I could be alive and never own a word.

When a local looked at me,
maybe I'd smile. Most times not.
Just walked. A little dangerous,

mine being the only face didn't
look like it was from somewhere.
Didn't know shit a face should.

The End of the World Cookbook

1.

Vista of mountains snow-topped too tall to believe
At the end of a runway broken hatch of an airplane like a single
    cast-off flower petal
Men in monochrome jerseys squatting at street corners
    spitting shells
Cheap orange sack filled with tomatoes and flat bread
Every apartment building socialized to look like every other
Horse hooves clip-clopping down main street screeching axles
    carts to market
Trucks lights banked smuggling petrol manhole covers
    missing
Nary a cat or an ice cube

2.

Unmarrieds in crisp blouses and old skirts brushed new the
    steel-pin pride of poverty and obsolescence
The trees along the roads whitewashed one pack of dogs
    howling chorus to another
Women little older than I folded in half sweeping the previous
    day from the streets
Women selling milk in green Mason jars
Women selling cigarettes in singles toasted sunflower seeds
    anything for a price
Dead refrigerators tricked out as cupboards a television like a
    plinth picture squashed flat into a gray soupy line
Kitchen gardens and ash heaps
Bus windows huzzahed shut in summer so no one gets the
    grippe

Orange plastic sacks for bread and for flour orange plastic sacks for cabbage and carrots and onions and tomatoes orange plastic sacks for raspberries cherries plums (oh the plums)
Radiators like defanged serpents silent all winter

3.

The telephone operators and/or prostitutes telephone booths stripped bare
The last living Armenian hawking roasted chicken legs spiced with sesame seeds
Flour in burlap sacks piled high inside the post office to pay the local teachers
Flawless blue Martian sky never troubled by contrails and a car horn honking a few bars of the love theme from *The Godfather*
Some pain never goes away
In the abandoned amusement park a jet's wings fringed with holiday lights
The smallest currency softened by anonymous hands and in a pinch employed as toilet paper
Trees the conquerors colonized none taller than two stories harvested of the unnecessary signaling hard times to come
A town called Sugar a girl named Sweetness

4.

Cheap orange sacks for blue test booklets for cigarettes and vodka for foreign chocolates and cut flowers trucked in from who knows where
Searching for matches in the rain toasting a hot dog over a candle flame hot sizzle mixed with wax

Told the Nazis invented Fanta and to detour any man splayed
   face down in the street
"Hotel California" and the Backstreet Boys and "Macarena"
   and Chekhov and Princess Di and irregular blackouts
Tire unspooling down a street and a jolly fat man giving chase
   bullying it back to his car wedging the tire on tootling off
Red haze of cooking fires at dusk

5.

After the first snow watching two children slide down a tiny
   rut from dawn to dinner
Only the brave or the foolhardy venturing out after dark
Hating this end of days (loving it too)
Every floor in every building in every town painted the same
   proletariat shade
Teller at a bank motioning me to follow her to the
   back pointing to a locker charity from overseas each
   compartment sparkling with a new combination lock
Teller asking please please to open laughing when I said
   without the combinations no one could.

Repair

Snow———the silence
                within silences———
a flickering streetlamp———her gloved hand———

Ремонт scrawled in Cyrillic on an abandoned shack———
the good-night kiss——— . . .

———then the small, fused heat of her
gone
       & me
racing to my flat———so fast I cannot drown———

—Jalal-Abad, Kyrgyzstan

Kairos

Two toughs who followed me up the stairwell
asked if I understood in a language I understood
well enough to know I should not understand.

The stairwell almost dark. Somebody had stolen
the selfsame light bulbs I might have found
and bought at the bazaar across the street.

Outside my flat before the rusted security door
anyone—a toddler even—could've ripped
from spalling concrete, one of the two unbuttoned

his coat and showed what they wanted me to see.
It might've been a toy, but the muzzle hole
looked real. He repeated if I understood.

I didn't respond, turning my back to open
my door. When I breathed again, when I was able
to look out the *glazok*, they were gone. History.

Seventieth Anniversary of the Revolution Street

This man, half Russian, he'd drop by my flat
unannounced and without asking rise
on tiptoe and reach for the top of my wardrobe
wide as a fat man's coffin
the sole piece of furniture the previous
tenants abandoned when after the collapse
of the USSR they fled north beyond the steppe
down he'd take one of the handful
of books I'd wrapped in perma-press shirts
and lugged halfway across the world
set it on his dusty knees like a spoiled orphan
books we agreed had big souls
those left now mostly elementary primers
for barter on fleece carpets
paper cheap and covers radiating
less harm than Winnie the Pooh or Hello Kitty
I didn't need him to tell me
what had been had been lost
most of the old books burned
not out of anger or hate or disbelief or politics
engineers like him had to sell
new potatoes and Coca-Cola in the bazaar
and it got cold mornings
with or without the statue of Lenin in the town square
eventually he'd open the book
where didn't matter he didn't read English
and he'd dip his nose in
breathing long and deep
the broken promises of paper and ink.

—*Jalal-Abad, Kyrgyzstan*

The Widower's Daughter

That it was an island is little matter.
At the seventh of seven villages, at the top
of the mountain, we stopped to see the caretaker

who spoke some English and lived a short walk
from the house where we'd spend the night.
We found him on his stoop, whittling a stick.

When he saw us, he disappeared inside
and returned smiling, with iced cans of beer.
We sat, and he told us the news, bit by bit,

between sips. At some point he called
through the door and his daughter brought
shallow bowls and spoons. Of the color

of her hair or eyes, the shape of her hands,
I remember nothing. I remember her soup.
White beans. Pinch of sea salt. Nothing more.

Mixed Martial Arts

It's the second horn alarms you.
The first could be a singularity, benign tumor
or prodigious skin tag. The second,
though misaligned and happily
for your self-esteem hidden behind a bang,
hints of a deeper, more Rosicrucian design.

Now you sport baseball caps, let sedans pricier
than yours cut you off
without an obscene oath or manic stab of the car horn.
Panhandlers view you as a softer touch.
To be safe you stay late at work and wait for your boss to leave.
Pay your credit off before you get the bill.

Watching your wife bend to slip flats on for yoga
you wonder. What of this newfound
fondness for sriracha and mixed martial arts?
Why this smell of brimstone everywhere,
even in the bedroom,
though neither of you has opened a pack of cigarettes for years?

Could a demiurge survive unrelenting emptiness?

When no one is looking you feel for the nascent horn
and, finding it, titter,
the prick of pain almost a pleasure.

The Event

That which
cannot happen
which
will not happen
which must
not happen
not here not
now not ever
the impossible
the unimaginable
factorless
unpredicted and unpredictable
and secretly wished for.

The Potato Eaters
—after Van Gogh

Love, in the beginning, you and I were purblind kittens
mauling each other
with milk teeth and Velcro paws.

Next, vipers, opium-laced, our liquid lives made knitting
and unknitting intricate and indecorous knots.
Lord, what lovely angles we did make.

Now as we sit and sup our dinner of Salisbury steak and tater tots
I contemplate how right it would feel
to Godzilla-stomp first one then the other kneecap

while you, if I know you truly, love,
calculate the launch velocity of a Himalayan-sized payload
intended to crater what's left of my good looks.

The Weekend Muses

Something in me,
about me,
genetic flaw or grace,
wants to think
one of the nine
must be sweet on me, only me.
Not the most
beautiful or most hip, but the one
with the soft spot
for possums
and public libraries.
Or the one
who haunts the graveyard shift,
rising before dawn
to unruffle the wrinkles
in her company blouse,
tic-tac-toeing uptown,
pocketbook flustered with bus transfers,
to punch a clock weekends
the woman
at the bagelry
with the sleepy eyes
and Mona Lisa smile
who when I order my dozen plain
includes a thirteenth,
an everything, hot from the oven,
special for me.

A Small Thing

A small thing, yes, I admit,
but so is waking your teenage daughter
so she makes first bell, that's a small thing, too,
but if you blow it, she misses the bus,
doesn't deliver her oral report on Bastille Day,
which admittedly she didn't want to anyway,
and because she never says another word
to you or her teacher, finishes with a D+,
which in turn leads her to give up French
and sign up for American Sign Language,
not a bad thing in and of itself,
don't get me wrong, and may one day
have unexpected positive outcomes,
but until said day will leave you to wonder
when she starts signing at you
in lieu of talking, a less-than-positive
immediate outcome, because your mind
slipped once more and you forgot
another small thing, reserving her prom dress
or not using a gender-neutral pronoun,
if she hadn't overslept and missed her class
you wouldn't be in Marseille, say, at a café,
with someone new and exciting, marveling
    at the painterly light.

How to Become a Clown

—after the title of a children's book

To begin: a clown simply is. He must
learn to mime the sorrow of trees, study
the big top of desire, expect no friend
but his own shadow. A clown paints both eyes
into bright buttons of pain, moistens his lips
with lost legal battles and whiskey bottles,
wears his Orange Julius hair long because
he misses his manic monkey tail. A clown
hums "America the Beautiful," sings the body
General Electric. A clown asks, *You just happy
to see me or is that a sixteen-wheeler I feel in
your pants?* To clown is to come one step closer
to Christ: salvation is where one finds it.
Another philosophical question: does one peel
or unpeel a banana? A clown talks national security,
our American empire of ghosts. He thinks,
I can do this in my sleep. A clown must learn
to smoke cigars in a bathtub, hobnob with lions
and mice. Play duets with wind-up novelty teeth.
Remember: a clown is the mortician of the soul.
To applause, a clown opines on a talk show,
*You can't change who you are, but you can change
who you become.* A clown prays, *Let no one
show me the door, I know the way.*

Heart Like a Dog

Heart like a dog wags its tail thump thump.
Heart like a dog just wants to be friends.
Heart like a dog isn't dangerous, forgive the growl.
Good heart like a dog.

Heart like a dog learns early how to beg and roll over and play dead.
Takes a beating but always returns home.
Heart like a dog never outgrows a fear of thunder and sirens and other dire pronouncements.
Heart like a dog can't carry a tune.
Writes love poems with fill-in-the-blanks, kites checks it can't cash.
Lives for the rhythm of the sun and the hole in the world the wind makes.

Heart like a dog can hold its drink. Until it can't.
Heart like a dog shits its bed and licks itself after.
Is a sucker for a scratch behind the ear, the purr of its own name, for hubcaps and butterflies and other bright things.
Heart like a dog will hump whatever will stand for it.
Searches and searches for an itch it can't scratch.
Trust me, heart like a dog is a metaphysician, pragmatist, romantic, solipsist, eroticizer, optimist, cynic, cad.

Be grateful I tell my heart.
Be grateful for all you have and little you really need, for the what-fors and might-have-beens.
Be grateful for the hurt that does not unduly scar you.
For other people's lies, in that they reveal in you the truth.

Watch heart like a dog as it slumbers: legs atwitch dreaming
   of running and running and never quite getting.
Heart like a dog knows how to open doors, not how to close
   them.
Nor ever fully fathoms what should be dug up, what should be
   left behind.

Jesus H. Christ

Jesus never had to stand behind a dog,
plastic bag in hand, counting to ten.

Never got to skip or juggle oranges
or unclog a plugged sink. Never

hocked a loogie from the railing of an overpass.
Hard to imagine him scratching his nuts

or sniffing the armpit of his best pinstripe
on the suburban rail at rush hour.

What was he beneath his halo,
those thorns he suffered for?

Don't know about you
but after I do the totally numbskull—

what he by thirty-three never could've—
forget my wallet or jam baby toe against bedpost,

cursing his mother-bleeping name,
I'm there with him, on the road to Golgotha,

all of us—centurions, thieves, hoi polloi, God—
shutting our eyes for a few heartbeats,

letting him whistle a scrap of song,
savor the smallest skip or two.

Scow

My ship's finally come in, except it ain't
the sleek beauty I half-hoped for. It's a scow,
yes, you know, those maritime eyesores mucking
their way up the seams of gridlocked waterways,
shepherds to the dredged, salvaged, feckless. Rancid,
the color of mudslide, berth to sea rat and barnacle.
Reeking of sewage and bilge water, overworked
inboard belching recycled motor oil and hellfire,
elegant as a snowplow on a dance stage, broad-beamed
babushka hip-checking a path through a flea market.
In sum, a moveable landfill, seaworthy as a tennis shoe.
O, but it's mine, all mine, my sweet Mary Celeste,
this poem a flag I'll unfurl come sunrise before all
the gods of the deep, my pledge always to adore it.

Letting Go

Though you could throw it away,
what is it but a dish, you color
the chip in the bowl's lip with marker.

You save the wedge of lemon,
a used tea bag. The mushrooms
in the fridge grow mushrooms.

The fear of giving up, of giving in.
How's that working for you,
your therapist says, as she unbinds

her ponytail, shakes it out,
then gathers it together
to make what's old new again.

The Unnumbered Anniversaries

Like the rain

Like the purr of the furnace

Like the half-empty laundry basket and the yellowing lamp glow of the house across the street

Like the sure flight of a small bird

Like the calligraphy behind your eyelids. The promise of onions frying

Like a man walking the dog (or the dog walking a man)

Like the sacred space just before sunrise

Like a picture frame but without the picture

Like a neighborhood and like the same neighborhood a heartbeat later

Like happiness, but not quite

Like sadness, too

Like a blue door

The morning you gave up caring

The Correct Use of Each Other

Talking about dead pets, Stephanie, the woman from Tulsa,
told me about her parakeet and how she'd kept it in her freezer,
between the lima beans and broccoli, neither of which she liked,

how she had bought the parakeet as a surprise for her husband,
and how the parakeet one second was chirping on his shoulder
and the next he was collapsed on the floor dead of a stroke.

Something about hockey and women, they don't mix,
like another time I was a junior in high school and took a senior
with the sweetest eyelashes to a game and between periods,

while others went for refills or a stale package of Twizzlers,
I handed her a Valentine's horror story I'd written for her,
though I never told her, and how when finished she pulled

a pen from her purse and started to mark up the story,
explaining when to use "each other" and when "one another,"
and how later after my folks picked us up and left me

to escort her to the door for what I'd hoped would be a kiss
instead ended up an invitation into the glare of her living room,
her mom boiling us green tea and her telling me about

John 14:6 and her personal relationship with Christ.
All I wished was to be with my parents, in the back seat
of our car, far from this or any other living room, wished I didn't

face a long, icy walk home, just as I'm sure Stephanie
from Tulsa wished she'd never put the parakeet in her freezer,
wished she'd resisted the urge to buy the thing in the first place,

her husband laughing and with her now, and not found herself in a funky-smelling arena in Boston, with a temp with whom she'd shared an office for all of two days, talking about dead pets.

Dishes

I drive to a fish farm where a man in Lederhosen escorts me through a hall of fish tanks. Afterward he brings me to a small pond and hands me a quarter for pellets from a gumball machine. Looking into the pond is like falling through a mirror in a funhouse. As instructed, I throw a pellet in, then casually pocket the rest. At home I underhand one into the sink and step back and let the dishes thrash around a while.

Drone

      How about that weather friend
between the experience of living a normal life How about that
weather friend *at this moment* How about that weather
friend *on the planet* How about that weather friend
  and the public narratives being offered How about that
   weather friend *to give a sense to that life*
   How about that weather friend *the empty space*
   How about that weather friend *the gap is enormous*
   How about that weather friend *the desolation lies*
  How about that weather friend *there* How about
that weather friend *not in the facts* How about that
   weather friend *this is why we are ready*
   How about that weather friend *to listen to* _____
   How about that weather friend *the story he tells*
  How about that weather friend *evil as it is is* How
     about that weather friend
closer to what is happening How about that weather friend
 in the streets this is why How about that weather friend
people dream How about that weather friend *of virtual
reality anything* How about that weather friend *from
 demagogy to manufactured* How about that weather
friend *dreams anything* How about that weather friend
 anything to close the gap How about that weather friend
in the gaps we get lost How about that weather friend *in
    the gaps we go*
   How about that weather friend *mad.*

November 9, 2016

The Lost Head of the Android Philip K. Dick

Without my head   I'm still Philip K. Dick
yet why do I dream so   Look

so many children   so many not crying
and that homeless man   What's he doing

using an omnibus of John Carter of Mars
as a pillow   I know they know   he knows

Just because something exists   doesn't mean
it's real

People keep walking   when they are
lost   What is this body   but

a buttonhole of time   biochemical latitudes
Find my head   save us all

Junkers

Pancaked, mashed, beaten, awaiting their eventual resurrection.

Tires blown off and fuming like the blowzy heads of dandelions.

Every radio tuned to the same dead-end frequency.

Accidents of Time and Space

If life can be likened to a plane flight—
gate first, then buckling up, tucking in,
an eerily familiar person up front telling you
what, where, when, how, but never why,
white knuckled at takeoff, suddenly
vertiginous until things settle down to
a steady thrum and you reach an altitude
your shoes no longer cinch so tight and you
can get up and walk about or stare at clouds,
the food often unpalatable, and turbulence
makes you quit whatever you're doing,
peer deep into other faces, the movies you swear
you'll view again on the big screen one day,
small talk about a sick aunt or local sports star
with the neighbor, then the gradual descent,
the relief, how else to describe it, the voyage
almost over and a prayer the landing will be
a soft one—if so, also true you arrive
at the same airport you took off from
and the keys you pat your pockets madly for
you don't have now, nor had to begin with.

Poem

You tell it
knowing in telling it
you'll get it wrong
put the stress
in the wrong place
miss the pothole in the shallows
which is why
you must tell it
again knowing
you're sure
to make a wrong
exit in the same place
or more likely
some new screw up
so you keep telling
and telling it until
if you're lucky
the missteps become
the telling it
and you can stop.

The In-Joke

is the best
joke

hurting
no one
who matters

though there's always
the risk
make it too private

you'll wake up
bloody lip & bruised
knuckles.

Love Poem

An artificial intelligence somewhere
is writing this poem and writing it better.
Images truer, the voice not so limited

and identifiably mine, and what your eyes
are compared to neither hackneyed nor trite
but laid out in meter and perfectly rhymed

and, if read backward, encrypted in code
for a fleet of ballistic missiles siloed
and go for launch in distant North Dakota.

No Matter What

The chicken as chicken
sees you and the you
behind you you cannot see
not being blessed with
chicken eyes or brain
or chicken spleen and god
forbid not tasting like chicken
no matter what third-grade
bully or senior exec outside
teak-paneled boardroom
or laughing cannibals lip-
syncing in poison-dart rainforest
think or say and the chicken
that sees the you behind you
sees all without seeing.

Junk

In a musty shop where even a dream wouldn't go,
you find them under glass,
set on pink velveteen among other gewgaws,
Ron Padgett's glasses,
and in their depths, as in a fortune teller's ball,
you view neither yourself
nor a wet, leaf-strewn street in Paris, nor even
a pair of sleet-blue eyes.
What have you done to Ron Padgett?
you want to shout at the old woman behind the counter,
we need him!
                      But that's
no old woman,
it's a hat rack with a white furred hat snagged
on top, the type of hat
nobody'd be caught dead wearing anymore.

Cailloux

Though it might appear
a massive louche hand
shook and scattered them

onto a jeweler's cloth,
don't let their sly reticence
deceive: pebbles on the beach

let themselves be pocketed.
Unlike the pitiless light
illuminating them, they remain

emphatically themselves
no matter how far
or fast they travel: a fish bowl

on the mantel, forgotten
in a pocket of ripped jeans,
or, say, in the foreground

of a small canvas by a Flemish master
before which a tearful young
woman recites Reverdy.

Signals

The character I call *I* wants to thank
the character who doesn't exist

who phoned in a dream to tell me
what I must do with my life

which is why I find myself packed
and in my car on my way to a city

the character I call *I* has never seen before,
except online and on TV, and thus

will remain as made up until I arrive
as the character who doesn't exist

I want to thank who has just awakened
and even though he can't fathom why

he'd phone a person he's never met
he feels so good, whatever he said,

when he enters the kitchenette he gives
his imaginary wife a hearty kiss,

the aroma of make-believe espresso
and sizzle of faux bacon lingering

in his mind like a half-forgotten song
so when he doesn't make the morning's first signal

he looks over at the driver in the next lane
and before the light changes

gives him a merry nod and then accelerates off
to the city where dreams go

leaving the character I call *I* to wonder
what the heck that was all about.

Make Like Shakespeare

Never mind the infinite number of monkeys punching
away at a like number of Cold War era typewriters,

picture instead the dented garbage cans
emptied by an inexhaustible rotation of janitors,

the sinks in countless incorporate bathrooms overflowing,
phalanxes of entry-level shlubs assigned

to just swing out and pick up a rain forest's worth
of paper, typewriter ribbon, Red Bull, bananas, only after

begging petty cash from zombie-eyed accountants.
Not to mention the looped Muzak, genital scratching

and union dues, crumpled coffee cups, message lights
blinking overtime on a gazillion cloned phones,

by each keyboard, framed pix of significant other
and/or kids requiring eons of orthodontia.

Dead lottery tickets, chewing gum, get-well cards
and sticky notes, pints of forbidden hooch,

played out against the glow of neon bulbs flickering off
to a point that never quite manages to vanish,

all to produce, by pure chance, an exact copy of *Hamlet*
or *King Lear* or, almost surely, this very poem wilting

in your inbox that ends with a monkey-minded flourish
the Bard himself might've enjoyed if not employed:

Time flies like an arrow, fruit flies like a banana.

Gnomic

—after William Bronk

The long and tall never are.
Leave it to the lonely
who take their blessings small
to say what cannot but is,
and not what can be but isn't.

Sixty Pieces of Word

The poem you read now
you will forget
and is designed to be
whereas most
aspire otherwise

The poem you read now
is pragmatic shameless
no simile to rustle memory
no metaphor to provoke
lost feeling

The poem you read now
started at the top of the page
will fulfill its function
and now end nowhere
you need ever remember

More about Me

Viewed from the proper angle, that is
the perspective of its putative owner,
my big toe, that which doesn't align
precisely with the dictionary definition,

resembles, thanks to injury, arthritis,
bunged nail, nothing less than bottlenose
dolphin. At moments of its own choosing,
often when most unexpected, I encounter it

bobbing just beyond the final fluffy wave
of the down comforter, mouth ajar,
peering up at me in its dolphiny way,
with what might be a toothy smirk

or shit-eating grin, as if it could tell
so much more about me it never will.

Note to an Old Friend

I'd like to say, to explain this thirty-year silence,
there was, in no particular order, a car wreck,
short-term amnesia, a bad marriage, the recession,
a loss of several jobs, three months on the sixth floor
of a hospital drying out, a stint on the Amazon,
a Wall Street deal gone bust, the loss of several more jobs,
shingles, a second marriage worse than the first,
no children but a three-legged dog, a rapprochement
with God, country, and family, a penthouse bungalow.
Even if I could assure you no one in this telling
was harmed, not even me, all of it would be a lie,
no, a series of ever more contradictory fabrications
like those made up when I missed midnight curfew
or came home buzzed, an irreparable ding in the fender,
the silence of these thirty years, I'd have to say,
explained more by what didn't happen than what did,
the small gestures, the daily wins v. losses, like old scars
now invisible, minutes stretching into hours, weeks, years,
adding up to a life I look back on now and wonder.

God on the Roof

About getting old, there's less laundry to do.
Imagine growing up in a town that only made gloves
or shirt collars. Sometimes it's okay not to speak
in sentences. Were there non sequiturs before
the Romans? Just when you think you know,
Poof! Or imagine you saw a god on the roof
across the alley nailing down new shingles all day.
I'm not sure what to think about the magnetic poles
and the fact they're moving, but what if rats wrote
their own history? The leftovers may have my name
on them, but I'm not really sure why anymore.

Or Not

You chew what's in your mouth,
chew as you were taught to chew—
thirty times, forty times. The less
to swallow, the more to chew.
Your job to chew what's there
until what's what is too immaterial
to lodge in teeth, lurk beneath
the tongue, nothing dark to brush,
spit out, and watch swirl down
the drain. You keep chewing—
three hundred, four hundred times—
masticating, manducating, triturating,
other synonyms you've never known,
in languages still to be invented,
mandible piston-like, unrelenting,
except for an occasional tensile pop.
Like stamping sheet metal, like
machining product on an assembly line,
except what's produced is annihilation,
is presence commuted to absence.
Chew. Chew as you were taught.
Only nothing will make you stop.

At a Certain Age

This poem keeps me here
living, today, another day.
Just as the next will
and one after that.

And so on, not for infinity
of course but for some days
beyond which it's thankfully
still difficult to calculate.

I'm old enough to believe,
but not so old,
and believing I know now,
in itself, is enough.

And even if wrong,
and I may be,
grant me this kindness.
Just as the old hand unspools line

after the rainbow bites,
gives it some run for a while.
Lets its big wild heart
wear its ragged self out.

What I've Learned Living on Other Planets

Some places look better on calendars.

*

You're never really alone in a forest.

*

Avoid destinations where even the clouds lack character.

*

A bed is only for sex and sleep.

*

Dogs are universal; cat's not so much.

*

Universal rarely really applies.

*

Don't pee in bathtubs, no matter how tempted.

*

Magic is ultimately about death and faith.

*

Heliotrope is a word only poets or archfiends use.

*

Never travel with anyone who says, "Wake me when we get there."

*

Alphabetize your socks and pack a spare water bottle.

*

Remember: all mathematics are subjective.

*

Nowhere is it good form to begin a sentence, "Where I come from..."

*

Remember: what holds us together are the weak forces.

*

At some point, you will thank God whether you believe or not.

Heron

We need you
to welcome day.

Where you
come from,

where you go,
without you,

your obdurate perpendicularities,
the world

turns
less substantial,

an ink wash painting
from which we

need not wake

Notes

1 The italicized text in "Drone" is adapted from John Berger's essay "A Man with Tousled Hair."

2 "The Lost Head of Philip K. Dick" riffs off the story that Hanson Robotics activated an android version of Dick in 2005. The android was subsequently lost on a flight from Dallas to San Francisco later the same year. Dick died in 1982.

Acknowledgments

I would like to express my sincere gratitude to the following journals where poems in this collection have appeared or are forthcoming:

Anacapa Review: "Anecdotes"
Another Chicago Magazine: "To Goya," "How to Become a Clown," "A Small Thing," and "Dishes"
Appalachian Review: "Wildflowers" and "Poem"
The Avenue: "The Regular"
BigCityLit: "Love Poem"
Cincinnati Review: "Sixty Pieces of Word"
Compass Rose: "Seventieth Anniversary of the Revolution Street"
Comstock Review: "Cailloux"
Connecticut River Review: "Livelihoods"
descant: "All the Time in the World" and "Accidents of Time and Space"
Dunes Review: "Catch"

Hole In The Head Review: "Namesake: An Elegy" and
    "Signals"
Ibbetson Street: "Mixed Martial Arts"
Iconoclast Literary Magazine: "The Weekend Muses"
I-70 Review: "What the Chaplain Saw" and "Scow"
Main Street Rag: "Letting Go," "More About Me," and
    "Heron"
New Plains Review: "The Event"
North Dakota Quarterly: "My Presidents," "The End of the
    World Cookbook," and "Make Like Shakespeare"
Ocotillo Review: "Jimmy Olsen"
OxMag: "The Unnumbered Anniversaries" (as "Like")
Paterson Literary Review: "The Best of a Bad Year"
Poet Lore: "Saved"
Rust & Moth: "The Widower's Daughter"
San Pedro River Review: "The Bird Watcher"
Schuylkill Valley Journal: "La Vida Loca"
Sierra Nevada Review: "The Correct Use of Each Other"
SLANT: "To Loss"
Sonora Review: "Repair"
South Carolina Review: "Heart Like a Dog" and "Note to
    an Old Friend"
Stonecoast Literary Review: "Junk"
Third Wednesday: "What I've Learned Living on Other
    Planets"
Tipton Poetry Journal: "Nobody's," "God on the Roof," and
    "At a Certain Age"
Two Thirds North: "Chevrolet Tango"

"The Best of a Bad Year" also was featured in the anthology *When Home Is Not Safe: Writings on Domestic Verbal, Emotional and Physical Abuse* (McFarland, 2021).

Thanks to all the folks who've given me encouragement and support over the years. If you've managed to get this far in the book, you know who you are.

Special props, in no particular order, to Jem Gaies, Duncan Basson, Jack McCarthy, Nancy Naomi Carlson, Nabil Chemaly, Betsy Marcotte and Lloyd Feinberg, Jean Grow and Mark Kuehn, Michael and Pat Libling, Danuta Kosk-Kosicka and Andrzej Kosicki, Eric Muhr and the Fernwood team, Peter Reiss, Judy Skillman, Greg Berger and Katie Klimowicz, and, of course, my family.

About the Author

Kurt Olsson has published two previous award-winning collections of poetry, *Burning Down Disneyland* (Gunpowder Press) and *What Kills What Kills Us* (Silverfish Review Press). His poems have appeared in *Poetry, The New Republic, Southern Review, The Threepenny Review,* and many other journals. Currently, he is pursuing a doctoral degree in English at the University of Wisconsin–Milwaukee.

Title Index

A
- Accidents of Time and Space 58
- All the Time in the World 21
- Anecdotes 31
- A Small Thing 44
- At a Certain Age 74

C
- Cailloux 64
- Catch 25
- Chevrolet Tango 14

D
- Dishes 54
- Drone 55

E
- Ephemera 19

G
Gnomic 68
God on the Roof 72

H
Heart Like a Dog 46
Heron 77
How to Become a Clown 45

I
Incredible Journey 18

J
Jesus H. Christ 48
Jimmy Olsen 17
Junk 63
Junkers 57

K
Kairos 37

L
La Vida Loca 16
Letting Go 50
Livelihoods 27
Love Poem 61

M
Make Like Shakespeare 67
Mixed Martial Arts 40
More about Me 70
My Presidents 30

N
Namesake: An Elegy 24
Nobody's 32

No Matter What 62
Note to an Old Friend 71

O
Or Not 73

P
Poem 59

R
Repair 36

S
Saved 15
Scow 49
Seventieth Anniversary of the Revolution Street 38
Signals 65
Sixty Pieces of Word 69

T
The Best of a Bad Year 13
The Bird Watcher: An Elegy 26
The Correct Use of Each Other 52
The End of the World Cookbook 33
The Event 41
The In-Joke 60
The Lost Head of the Android Philip K. Dick 56
The Potato Eaters 42
The Regular 28
The Unnumbered Anniversaries 51
The Weekend Muses 43
The Widower's Daughter 39
To Goya 29
To Loss 22

W
What I've Learned Living on Other Planets 75
What the Chaplain Saw 23
Wildflowers 20

First Line Index

A

About getting old, there's less laundry to do 72
An artificial intelligence somewhere 61
A small thing, yes, I admit 44
A warm spring evening, after the grill closes 15
A young man, little more than a boy, sobs in back 22

E

Everyone in the room, even the cats,
    everyone in the house 16

H

Heart like a dog wags its tail thump thump 46
He's Bill, that's all 28
He was a punter, not the British kind,
    though he'd have liked that 24
How about that weather friend 55

I
I didn't know shit. I knew 32
I'd like to say, to explain this thirty-year silence 71
I drive to a fish farm where
    a man in Lederhosen escorts me 54
If art is the two sons of the famous lithographer 29
If life can be likened to a plane flight 58
I hated that dog the week it followed me 18
In a musty shop where even a dream wouldn't go 63
is the best 60
It's the second horn alarms you 40

J
Jesus never had to stand behind a dog 48
John F. Kennedy left me parched and sweat-soaked 30

L
Like the rain 51
Love, in the beginning, you and I
    were purblind kittens 42

M
My ship's finally come in, except it ain't 49

N
Never mind the infinite number
    of monkeys punching 67

P
Pancaked, mashed, beaten, awaiting their eventual 57

R
Remember when men smoked pipes 14

S

She loved birds, their secret logic.
   She went for long walks 26
Snowed only once 13
Snow   the silence 36
Some carry a piece of the cross with them 27
Some places look better on calendars 75
Something in me 43

T

Talking about dead pets, Stephanie,
   the woman from Tulsa 52
That it was an island is little matter 39
That which 41
The character I call I wants to thank 65
The chicken as chicken 62
The first writing class told us not 20
The first year, students would come up to me 31
The long and tall never are 68
The poem you read now 69
There was a time after I shoved a bean up my nose 19
This man, half Russian, he'd drop by my flat 38
This poem keeps me here 74
Though born with the fear of falling 21
Though it might appear 64
Though you could throw it away 50
To begin: a clown simply is. He must 45
Two toughs who followed me up the stairwell 37

V

Viewed from the proper angle, that is 70
Vista of mountains snow-topped too tall to believe 33

W

We need you 77
What he saw he never saw 23
Why perhaps as mundane as the shared last name 17
Without knowing you practice beauty 25
Without my head   I'm still Philip K. Dick 56

Y

You chew what's in your mouth 73
You tell it 59

www.ingramcontent.com/pod-product-compliance
Lightning Source LLC
Chambersburg PA
CBHW010046090426
42735CB00020B/3405